Dandelion, My House Chicken, *written by photograph< enthusiast Kim Carr, is a sheer delight to read. In this cho vibrantly illustrated with a painterly hybrid of Carr's own photography and creative filters, we are invited to a behind-the-scenes glimpse of life on a farm inhabited by cows, chickens, ducks, dogs, and a rock-star house chicken named Dandelion.*

Carr, having graduated college with an Animal Science degree, made her dream of owning a farm a reality when she settled onto a 20-acre property in mid-Missouri. Her passions for photography and animals have melded together to create a heartwarming, educational, and downright funny glimpse into the life of an animal lover and artist. Carr's love of nature and the many "critters" that inhabit this world may originate from her own backyard, but the life lessons she has learned on the farm resonate with a unique perspective, as do the universal truths about pursuing one's passions, the hard work it takes to forge them into reality, and the deep connections we can experience with the world around us—especially if you have an extraordinary house chicken named Dandelion by your side.

– Elizabeth Gracen—actress and owner of the online magazine FlapperPress.com and director/producer for Flapper Films

Told from the perspective of a real-life farmer, Dandelion: My House Chicken *is the true story of an unlikely friendship between a chicken and a duck. This would be a wonderful mentor text for a reading and writing workshop, or for your next read-aloud. Students will experience farm life through Kim's unique blend of storytelling and illustrations! Your students will enjoy this rich, expository text that includes vocabulary, definitions, and discussion questions throughout!*

– Emily Ngui, M.Ed.

Dandelion
my house chicken

Kim Carr

Dandelion, my house chicken

Kim Carr

Hybrid Hollow Production

Published by Hybrid Hollow Production, New Florence, MO

Photo illustrations: Kim Carr

Cover and Interior design: Creative Publishing Partners, Creative Publishing Partners.com

Names: Carr, Kim, 1963- author.

Title: Dandelion : my house chicken / Kim Carr.

Description: New Florence, MO : Hybrid Hollow Production, [2023] | Interest age level: 000-012. | Summary: Can you imagine what it would be like to have a pet chicken in your house? What do they like to eat? Are they neat housemates or messy? Are they quiet at night? Follow this fun and educational journey of Dandelion and her duckling best friend Buttercup from hatchlings to adulthood.--Publisher.

Identifiers: ISBN: 979-8-9873054-0-9 (paperback) | LCCN: 2022922008

Subjects: LCSH: Chickens--Juvenile literature. | Ducklings--Juvenile literature. | Pets--Juvenile literature. | Birds--Development--Juvenile literature. | Farm life--Juvenile literature. | CYAC: Chickens. | Ducks. | Pets. | Birds--Development. | Farm life. | BISAC: JUVENILE NONFICTION / Animals / Farm Animals. | JUVENILE NONFICTION / Lifestyles / Farm & Ranch Life. | JUVENILE NONFICTION / Animals / Pets.

Classification: LCC: SF487.5 .C37 2023 | DDC: 636.5--dc23

2023

Dedicated to the memory of my mom, who loved life on the farm almost as much as reading. I know she would be very proud to see this book come to life.

To my great nephew Brycen.

I'm looking forward to sharing many more adventures with you.

Love, Aunt Kim

Hello there! My name is Kim, and this is my pet chicken, Dandelion

Hello there! My name is Kim. Welcome to Hybrid Hollow Farm! I have a lot of animals that I care for every day. Being a farmer means I have lots of great stories from around the farm. I would like to share a true story with you about a very special chicken and her friends.

Living in the country, you never know what adventures will happen around the farm. Having an assortment of farm animals to care for is a lot of work, but it is also a lot of fun. I start each morning by doing my chores. Feeding the chickens and ducks, collecting eggs, watering the cows—these are just some of the farm chores that I must do every day to take care of my critters.

OH MY…Newly hatched, a baby duck
has fallen from his nest.
What will happen to him?

September

One morning, while doing my chores, I hear a very nervous "chirp chirp chirp … chirp chirp chirp". Upon investigating, I find the sound is coming from a baby duck who was all alone and scared. It's sitting at the base of a big oak tree in the front yard.

I look up at the tree and can barely see the momma duck. She is sitting on her nest tucked between the trunk and two large branches. It's too high up for me to safely return the baby duck to its nest without putting myself and the baby in harm's way. I'm worried about the baby's safety, being all alone on the ground without its mom to protect it. I know I need to act quickly before the baby wanders off by itself where it might be in danger. To keep the baby safe, I set up a temporary holding pen. I hope the mom will leave the nest soon with her other babies, and the family can be reunited. Have you ever been lost? It can be very scary—for baby ducks too.

As I finish making sure the baby duck is safe for the time being, I hear more excessive chirping. "Chirp chirp chirp … chirp chirp chirp". This time the noise is coming from the horse trailer. I peek in the door, and what do I see? A newly hatched baby chick. All well and good, except the baby chicken has been hatched by a DUCK!

This happens sometimes on the farm. My ducks and chickens will share a nest, laying their eggs in the same box or nesting area. I try to collect chicken eggs from the duck nest and vice versa, but sometimes I miss an egg or a nest. A momma chicken will do okay raising baby ducks; the problem comes when a momma duck hatches a baby chicken. Can you guess why this is a problem? Chickens don't swim! Once a momma duck has hatched all her eggs, she likes to head to the pond for a swim. This leaves the baby chicks alone on the pond bank and vulnerable to predators like hawks and coyotes. When the momma duck goes in for a swim, it causes quite the panic for any baby chicks left ashore because they are alone and not able to swim.

Momma ducks often pull their soft down feathers to line their nest. This helps insulate the eggs and exposes the mom's skin, which allows her to provide more body heat to the eggs during incubation. Baby ducks are born with webbed feet, which act like flippers. Plus, their feathers are waterproof, which allows them to float on the top of the water. Chickens do not have webbed feet, their feathers are not waterproof, and once the feathers are soaked with water, they will sink and not float. Chickens are landlubbers.

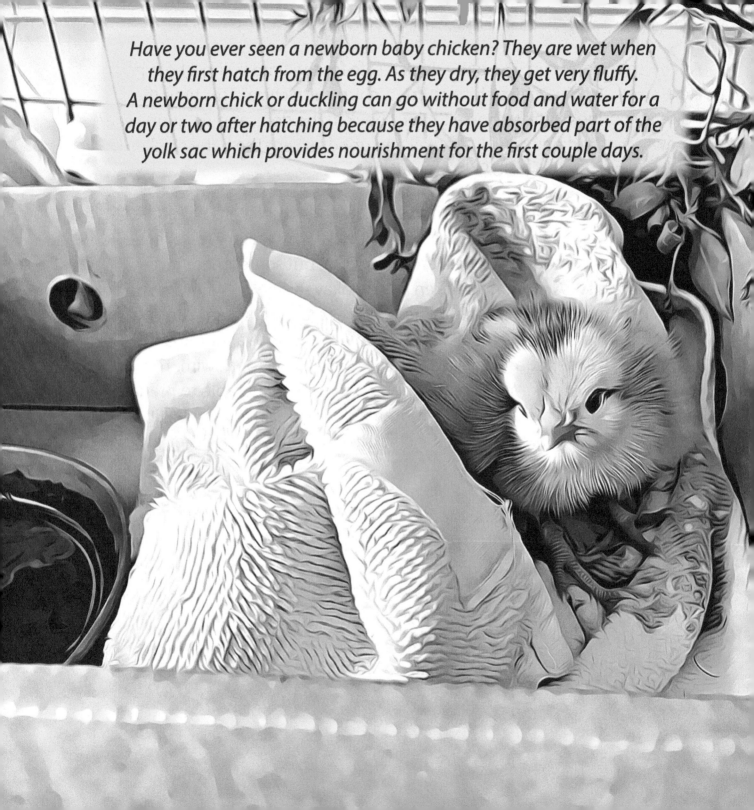

Have you ever seen a newborn baby chicken? They are wet when they first hatch from the egg. As they dry, they get very fluffy. A newborn chick or duckling can go without food and water for a day or two after hatching because they have absorbed part of the yolk sac which provides nourishment for the first couple days.

I know I need to act now for this baby chick to survive. I wrap her in a towel to dry and warm her. It's time to find a solution to this problem. Walking around the farm, I go into each of the chicken houses looking for a hen that might adopt this newly hatched chick, but no such luck. In the past, I have had success putting a new baby with another mom. Some hens are just exceptional at being a mom. They will accept and raise a new baby as their own. Unfortunately, I don't have any hens that have recently hatched any eggs. I set up a wire cage to place the baby in as I try to figure out what to do.

Throughout the day I keep checking on the baby duck in the front yard. I've placed it in a crate to keep it safe. I'm hoping the momma duck will come to the ground and reunite with her baby; however, she still has eggs to hatch. As it gets later in the day, it becomes obvious the momma duck is not leaving her nest today. Normally, all the eggs will hatch within a day or two of each other, but for some reason this baby duck has hatched earlier than the rest of the eggs. I'm not sure if he grew impatient and jumped from the nest or if he accidently got too close to the edge and fell.

Was it fate that I found both babies on the same day? It only seems natural that I raise them together. Time to bring these two into the house to raise until they are old enough to be on their own. What kind of pets do you share your home with?

Despite their differences,
this is the start of a great friendship.

Buttercup & Dandelion 1 day old

As a kid, I had pet mice, gerbils, and hamsters. With my allowance money from doing chores around the house, I would buy different Habitrail pieces. Habitrail is the little plastic tubes and houses you connect to create awesome climbing trails for your critters. I would change up the configuration all the time to create new trails. My favorite was when I built them to extend over my bed, and I literally had to slide in under the tubes to go to sleep at night. What fun watching and listening to my critters scamper about climbing, sliding, and running through the tubes. Even the squeaky wheel was music to my ears.

Now, as an adult, I find myself sharing my bedroom with more critters, only this time it's a baby duck and chicken instead of the pet rodents I had as a kid. Using the power of social media, I shared pics of my new babies on Facebook. I asked for help with naming this dynamic duo. A friend suggested Buttercup for the duck and Dandelion for the chick. These names seem to fit these little fluffballs, so it is now official: Buttercup and Dandelion. With the crate next to my bed, they have a heat lamp, water, food, and each other as company. Buttercup and Dandelion cuddle next to one another and slowly doze off. Just like I did as a kid, I find myself lying in bed watching and listening to these little critters sleep as I happily catch some Z's myself, knowing they are safe.

October

Amazing how fast baby ducks and chicks grow. These two have become quite the pair. Friends of a feather flock together. Sometimes they hang out on my desk when I am not too serious about getting much work done. It's all fun and games until one of them walks across my keyboard. They have been known to send emails full of gibberish … eee@+m0r3M3Alw0rmm$$' … Send Now … NOOO!

Take a close look at Dandelion. She is what is known as a Turken or a Naked Neck chicken. One of the characteristics of this breed is they lack any feathers on part of their neck. Sometimes people think something is wrong when they see a Turken or Naked Neck chicken, but it is just how this breed of chicken looks; they are perfectly fine and healthy. I love that she looks different from my other chickens. She is very distinguished looking, and her markings make her look like she has on eyeliner.

Of course, Buttercup really does look like a buttercup … huggable, squeezable, kissable, cute little chunk of a duck. Check out his claws though! Even at a young age, his claws are very sharp. Perhaps he needs a pedicure. I love my ducks and chickens. What is your favorite farm animal?

Ducks and Dogs and Cats, Oh MY!

Now that Dandelion and Buttercup are getting a little older, I have weaned them off the heat lamp that I used to keep them warm. Their feathers are growing in, and they can keep themselves warm by trapping their own body heat now. In nature, they would have huddled under their mom at night for warmth. Since I have played the role of their mom the past several weeks, I have used the heat lamp to help keep them warm. Guess I could tuck them under my arm to keep them warm when I go to bed—now THAT would be funny! Imagine having a chicken and a duck in your bed.

Hard to believe how fast Buttercup is growing—it's like lightning fast. He is outgrowing the wire crate in the house. See Buttercup peeking through the bars of the crate in the picture? My dog, Zak, and my cat, Pamela, don't mind sharing the house with a chicken and a duck. I just need to make sure there is plenty of room on my bed for Zak and Pamela or they would not be happy. No need for any jealousy here, plenty of room for us all.

Living on a small farm, over the years I've had a variety of critters in the house that needed special care. Can you believe, we've even had baby cows and lambs in the house who needed extra love and attention to get them started off on the right hoof? What would you think of a cow in your house?

Buttercup and Dandelion on bug patrol ... Yum, Yum.

With the babies growing, I set up a large dog kennel so Buttercup and Dandelion can go outside during the day. Here they run around on fresh grass and clover. Sunshine and fresh air are good for these youngsters, just like sunshine and fresh air are good for us. Now they can scratch and peck in the grass and dirt, and maybe they will even catch a couple bugs along the way or scratch up a worm or two for a tasty treat. Yum!

Many farmers keep ducks and chickens not only for the eggs they lay but because they are great at pest control. Bugs are a fun treat if Dandelion and Buttercup are fast enough to catch one. In addition to grain (cracked corn, sunflower seeds, oats) and laying crumbs, I put out mealworms for them to enjoy. Dandelion and Buttercup get very excited when they find a mealworm in the grass. Grabbing it in their beak, they take off running to keep the other one from grabbing it away. It's like a game of keep-away and the winner gets to eat the worm. DELICIOUS!

I hope winter doesn't get in a hurry to arrive. These two need more feathers and some more size before I set them loose in cold weather to free range the farm with the other birds.

At seven weeks of age, Buttercup and Dandelion are fearless as long as Zak and Marilyn are on guard duty.

November

With a window of nice weather, I made the leap a few nights ago and moved Buttercup and Dandelion outside permanently with the other ducks and chickens. It was like sending my kids on their first overnight stay at a friend's house. I didn't sleep well at all—headed outside twice in the middle of the night with a flashlight to check on them. To help them transition to life outdoors with the other farm birds, I set up a pen inside of a pen which allows them plenty of space to roam and roost at night while keeping them safe as they get accustomed to being outdoors 24/7.

Dandelion and Buttercup did just fine overnight and were excited to see me with their special treat of mealworms in the morning. Plan is to give them a couple days to acclimate to being outside day and night before setting them loose with the rest of the flock. Of all the lessons learned on the farm, one is … things seldom go as planned. You must be adaptable and able to change direction as needed. During the afternoon check, I notice Dandelion has escaped the pen but is hanging right outside the pen to be near Buttercup … who is still in the pen. Several adult birds are around, but no one is bothering Dandelion, who seems very content. I decide now is as good a time as any to open the gate and let Buttercup loose, too. My babies are growing up! They now have run of the farm just like the rest of my chickens and ducks.

Dandelion and Buttercup now roam the yard, so I work outside as much as possible to keep a close eye on them. I want to make sure they are not bullied by the older chickens and ducks. Most animals have a pecking order—that means someone is the boss and tends to lead the group. By keeping an eye on Dandelion and Buttercup, I can make sure they stay safe as they adjust to their new surroundings and the rest of the flock.

They are doing great wandering around the yard, not going too far from the safety of the porch, the chicken house and the dogs who keep a watchful eye out for all the farm animals. Late in the day, as the adult chickens and ducks start to go to roost, I gather up Buttercup and Dandelion and return them to their pen inside the chicken house. I continue to do this for a week or two until I feel comfortable knowing they will return to the chicken house to roost on their own at night.

I have a sheep named Poppy on the farm, and one day I was tickled to find Dandelion sitting on Poppy's back. If there ever was such a thing as a country Uber, I guess Poppy the sheep would be it. Have you ever seen a chicken riding a sheep? It's not the speediest transportation on the farm, but it's not baaaaad. Dandelion gives Poppy 5 out of 5 stars for her services.

Mealworms are a favorite treat for Dandelion and Buttercup. What is your favorite treat?

January

It is now January, and Dandelion and Buttercup are 14 weeks old, more than three months already! At this age, I think of them as young teenagers. See how much they have changed? Remember Buttercup was yellow as a little fellow? Look how handsome he is now with his bright white and shiny black feathers.

Chickens are considered mature at 18 weeks and may start laying eggs around six months of age. Ducks are mature around five months of age. As they have aged, you can see that their soft fluffy down has been replaced by feathers. Now you know why Dandelion and Buttercup are growing so fast.

If you want to see Dandelion and Buttercup come running, call out their names and have a handful of mealworms at the ready. Mealworms are dried larvae from the mealworm beetle. They are high in protein, which helps Dandelion and Buttercup with growing strong, beautiful feathers to keep them warm in the winter. They are also great for helping chickens regrow their feathers during molting season, which is when chickens shed their feathers and regrow new ones. The mealworms also help with egg production. Laying eggs is a lot of work; the extra protein helps to make a thicker shell and improves egg size and flavor. It won't be long before Dandelion starts laying eggs of her own.

Dandelion soaking up the sun on a wintery day.

February

Living in the Midwest—Missouri, to be more specific—means we have four seasons: winter, spring, summer and fall. Being a farmer means I spend a lot of time outdoors tending to my animals and taking care of the farm. It seems to me more like we have two seasons … winter, where it's really cold, and summer, where it's very hot. The animals tend to take these temperature changes better than I do. In the summer, I feel like I'm melting like butter on popcorn. In the winter, I feel like a frozen popsicle half the time. I love buttered popcorn and I LOVE red, white, and blue Bomb Pops, but my chores are still challenging. Fortunately, I LOVE my animals and I do LOVE being outdoors.

On hot days, the chickens and ducks seek out the shade. My cows like to stand in the pond to cool off. So, you see that the animals are very smart and find ways to handle the changing temperatures and weather. When I have time, I join my cows with a little paddle around the pond in my kayak.

On cold days in the winter, chickens and ducks stay warm because they are very warm blooded and fluff up their feathers to trap their body heat. The cows grow a thick coat to keep them warm.

Have you ever thought about building a snow chicken? You could pretend that snowballs are chicken eggs! Be careful of who you hit. Swoosh, splat!

To protect Dandelion from the extreme cold, I tucked her inside my coat to keep her toasty and warm.

When I go outside and it's very cold, I add extra layers of clothing—long johns, thick socks, knee high boots, facemask, hat, hoodie, coat, gloves, and I always keep an extra pair of gloves in my pocket in case the pair I'm wearing gets wet. Animals do not have the luxury of being able to add extra layers of clothing to stay warm. While their bodies will adjust to the changing weather, like my cows growing a thicker coat of hair, animals still need access to shelters or wind breaks to protect them from the weather. Farmers provide chicken houses, barns, and other ways for their animals to get out of the weather during all times of the year.

One morning while doing chores, I notice that with all the snow on the ground, Dandelion has gotten hung up in a snowbank. Most likely, she was trying to get away from the older hens who tend to chase her sometimes. Having been raised in the house and not by a momma hen, Dandelion is on the bottom of the pecking order. The older hens often chase Dandelion out of the chicken house during the day. Most days, this isn't a problem because she has other places to take shelter; however, with several inches of snow on the ground and the super cold temps, being outside unprotected is not a good thing. With the weather forecast calling for a big drop in temperature and chances of more snow, I decide it's time to bring my girl back inside the house. I swoop her up and carefully tuck her inside my coat to keep her toasty and warm.

My mom helps take care of Dandelion.
Does this make her a "Chicken Tender?"

Just outside the door, I stomp my feet, kicking the snow from my boots. Once inside, I holler for my mom who's in the kitchen. "Mom, Dandelion needs help!" I let my mom know that she is cold and damp from the snow. Mom always keeps a stash of towels handy just for the animals. Dandelion is not the first animal I've brought into the house for special care, and she won't be the last. Mom has a knack for taking care of critters in need.

I handed Dandelion over to Mom, who swaddled her in a towel, drying her and warming her chilly feet. I'm sure this isn't what my mom expected when she moved to the farm years ago. Guess she didn't read the fine print on the contract:" Must share house with an assortment of critters, tend to animals in need, dress wounds and nurse creatures back to health." She just dreamed of days on the deck watching the ducks swim back and forth on the pond while she sipped a lemonade. Certainly, all the animal care is just icing on the cake.

Once Mom has her warm and dry, Dandelion settles right back into life as a house chicken. The difference this time, she has free range of the house. No more confinement to a wire crate. I set up a wooden crate for her to roost on next to my desk. The wire crate she shared with Buttercup as a baby has been adapted and made into a food and water area for Dandelion. She is part of the family.

April

Now that spring has arrived, I have started letting Dandelion outside during the day. By late afternoon she comes back inside the house to spend the night. If the weather is bad, she stays inside where it is nice and comfortable year-round. The other chickens are more accepting of her now, perhaps because she is older, bigger, and better able to defend herself.

On a nice spring day, I have set Dandelion outside the door so she can go about her daily activities. It isn't long before she wants back in the house. Pacing back and forth in front of the sliding door, she is pecking at it like there is an urgency for her to come inside ... RIGHT NOW! I open the door, and she runs straight in the house to my bed where she promptly laid herself down, making herself nice and comfy.

She seems quite content laying on my bed, so I go back to doing my work. After a while, Dandelion starts cackling like she is making a big announcement ... "Bawk Bawk Bawk Bawk". In fact, she IS making a BIG ANNOUNCEMENT; Dandelion has laid her first egg!!! I feel like cackling too; this is an exciting day for us all. Say it with me now ... "Bawk Bawk Bawk Bawk". This is common behavior amongst hens, they like to sing out after laying an egg. It is indeed a happy noise. Just like clockwork, at six months of age, Dandelion has laid her first egg. It came as a bit of a surprise to her and me.

For a while, my bed has become the go-to place for Dandelion to lay her egg. I am amused by this. Each day, Dandelion knocks at the door, pacing back and forth to let me know she needs inside to lay her egg. Afterwards, she wants back outside to roam with the other chickens. Can't believe my baby is LAYING EGGS!!

Just to be safe, I decide I better create a nest box outside for Dandelion in case I'm not home when she needs to lay her egg. Now it seems everybody and her sister wants to use the new nest box. It's just a plastic container with a little bedding, nothing special, but the other birds sure are interested in it. There's a constant line of chickens and ducks waiting their turn to lay an egg in the new nest on the porch. I must admit, it's very nice to step out the door and collect fresh eggs for breakfast. Grocery shopping doesn't get any easier than this.

Chickens and ducks only lay one egg per day, but that doesn't mean that they lay an egg every day. It depends on the breed. Some breeds may only lay 30 to 60 eggs a year, some may lay 100 or more. The most productive chickens are White Leghorns; they may produce more than 300 eggs per year! Turkens or Naked Neck chickens like Dandelion, might lay 120-180 light-colored eggs per year. Now, I just need to make some bacon to go with these eggs.

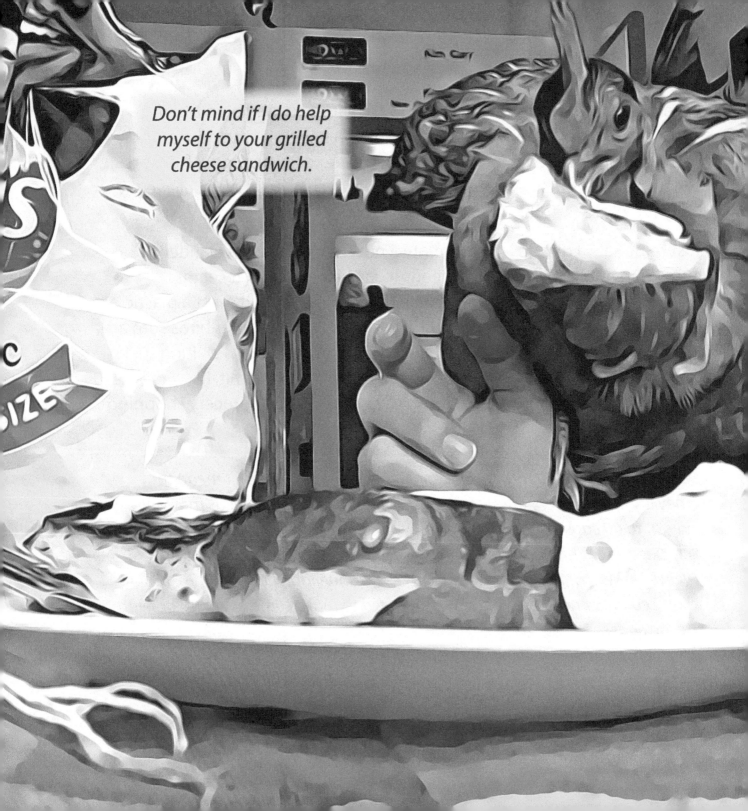

It's all fun and games having a house chicken until she tires of you tossing scraps on the floor for her to eat. When in the house, Dandelion has food and water bowls that she can help herself to at any time. Periodically, I toss mealworms on the floor so she can hunt and peck. Seems like she is always doing something funny. I tend to miss a lot of pictures because I am slow to get my phone out in time to capture all her antics. Today, I got lucky.

I was eating lunch, and Dandelion was sitting on her crate next to my desk. She was looking cute as she watched me eat. For grins, I snapped a picture or two of her, when suddenly Dandelion hops onto my desk and snatches part of my grilled cheese sandwich! Ha! Snapped a photo and caught her in the act! Thank goodness Mom has made me a sandwich and a half … plenty for me, and … plenty for Dandelion. Roaming the house is all fine and dandy, but she has terrible table manners. Very rude to snatch and fly. A please and thank you would have been nice. Would you share your lunch with a chicken?

Dandelion is now 8 months old. She likes to hunt bugs in the yard with Pickles the rooster.

May

Dandelion and Buttercup now are very independent but are still friends; they roam the same area on the farm and cross paths numerous times throughout the day. As they grow, both have made new friends, hanging out with other chickens and ducks. Most days, Dandelion can be seen roaming the yard with Pickles, the rooster, and a couple other hens. It's nice to see that she has other chickens to wander the yard with.

When Pickles was born, he was also hatched by a duck, just like Dandelion was. He was hatched the same time as another rooster, Pepper. Mom and I raised Pickles and Pepper in the house just like we did Dandelion and Buttercup. The only difference, once Pickles and Pepper moved outside with the other chickens, they **stayed** *out, free-ranging the farm during the day and going to roost at night in one of the chicken houses. Flip back towards the beginning of the book to see a picture of Pepper as a baby with his mom, Spice the duck.*

Dandelion certainly has the best of both worlds, being an indoor/outdoor girl. Her days are spent outside roaming the farm, and her nights safe inside wandering the house until bedtime.

She's some chicken.

Dandelion the free-range hen.
She is a super-hero amongst
the other farm animals.

Alamo Annie, Macaroni and Kiefer looking to see if I have any apples or pears to hand out.

In addition to chickens and ducks, I have a small herd of Irish Dexter cattle. Cows are curious creatures, especially the calves. They often come to the fence when I'm outside, especially if I'm near the fruit trees. These youngsters want to see if I have any treats for them. While they are not interested in the mealworms that I give to the chickens and ducks, they do love a good apple or pear. Last year, I fed over a thousand apples and pears to my small herd of Irish Dexters over the winter months. They make an excellent treat, so they bring the cows up close to the house so I can do a head count every day. "One cow, two cow, three …"

As the cows come up by the house, I can look them over to make sure everybody is in good shape. I do this with the other animals, too. When you have animals of any kind, you need to pay attention to how they look and act. You can tell a lot by their behavior and body condition. I do my best to make sure my animals are happy and healthy year-round. Keeping a close eye on them helps me make sure everybody is doing well.

Besides the cows, chickens and ducks, the wild rabbits and birds also love all the apples and pears that fall from the trees in autumn. My goal is to plant more fruit trees, creating a little orchard in the yard to share the fruit with my critters. Trees help make oxygen for you, me and the critters to breathe. They help create a healthy ecosystem providing shade, reducing erosion, creating homes for birds and other wildlife as well as food that we can enjoy, and I can share with my critters. Do you have any fruit trees or a garden in your yard?

Strange, now I'm hungry for a piece of apple pie.

Nothing to see here. Just a chicken laying an egg, in a dog bed, on the front porch. Perfectly normal, folks.

July

One day, Mom is sitting out on the deck reading a good book. She notices two eggs in one of the deck chairs that has a doggie bed in it for the cats. Apparently, this has become Dandelion's new go-to nest when laying her eggs outdoors. The line to use the plastic container is probably too long. Thank goodness people don't try to sit in this chair; they might be in for a surprise! Nobody wants to sit on a chicken egg other than a chicken … or a duck. Ha! That's how we got where we are, a duck sat on a chicken egg and now I have a pet chicken as a roommate!

The doggie bed in the deck chair has become Dandelion's favorite spot to lay her eggs when she is outside. With summer in full swing, Missouri has really cranked up the heat. To keep Dandelion cool and to make sure she is comfortable while laying her egg, I've placed a fan on the porch. Dandelion has come to enjoy the fan blowing on her as she sits on her doggie bed waiting to lay her egg. Some days she lays her egg quickly, other days she may sit in her chair an hour or two. The fan comes in handy keeping her cool and comfortable. She almost always sings her song of "Bawk Bawk Bawk Bawk", by clucking loudly for all to hear once she has laid her egg. I'm still just as excited as Dandelion; I just don't dance around the deck singing "Bawk Bawk Bawk Bawk". Actually, dancing is good exercise. Maybe I should give it a try.

September

It is now September; we celebrate Buttercup and Dandelion's one-year birthday! Look at Buttercup; he has grown to be a very handsome adult. I have carried Buttercup to the pond a couple times; he swims a little but readily makes his way back to the yard. Luckily, Muscovy ducks love being on land as much as they love the water. Buttercup is a true landlubber just like his sister, Dandelion. He spends his time wandering the yard with his fellow ducks hunting for bugs and begging me for mealworms whenever he gets the chance.

Male ducks are called drakes, and female ducks are called hens, just like a chicken. Muscovies are the largest of all domestic ducks, and easily identified by the red wattles around their beak and face. They are a quackless breed. Muscovies hiss and make other sounds, but they don't quack. The females are good egg layers and excellent mothers. Muscovies are also excellent flyers and will often roost in trees, on roofs or other high areas which helps keep them safe at night from predators like coyotes and bobcats.

At first, when I moved Buttercup and Dandelion outside, they spent time together. In time, they have started hanging out more and more with other critters like themselves. Here on the farm, everybody lives together and gets along. The trick is to have plenty of space for everyone to roam and do their own thing where they are happy and feel safe.

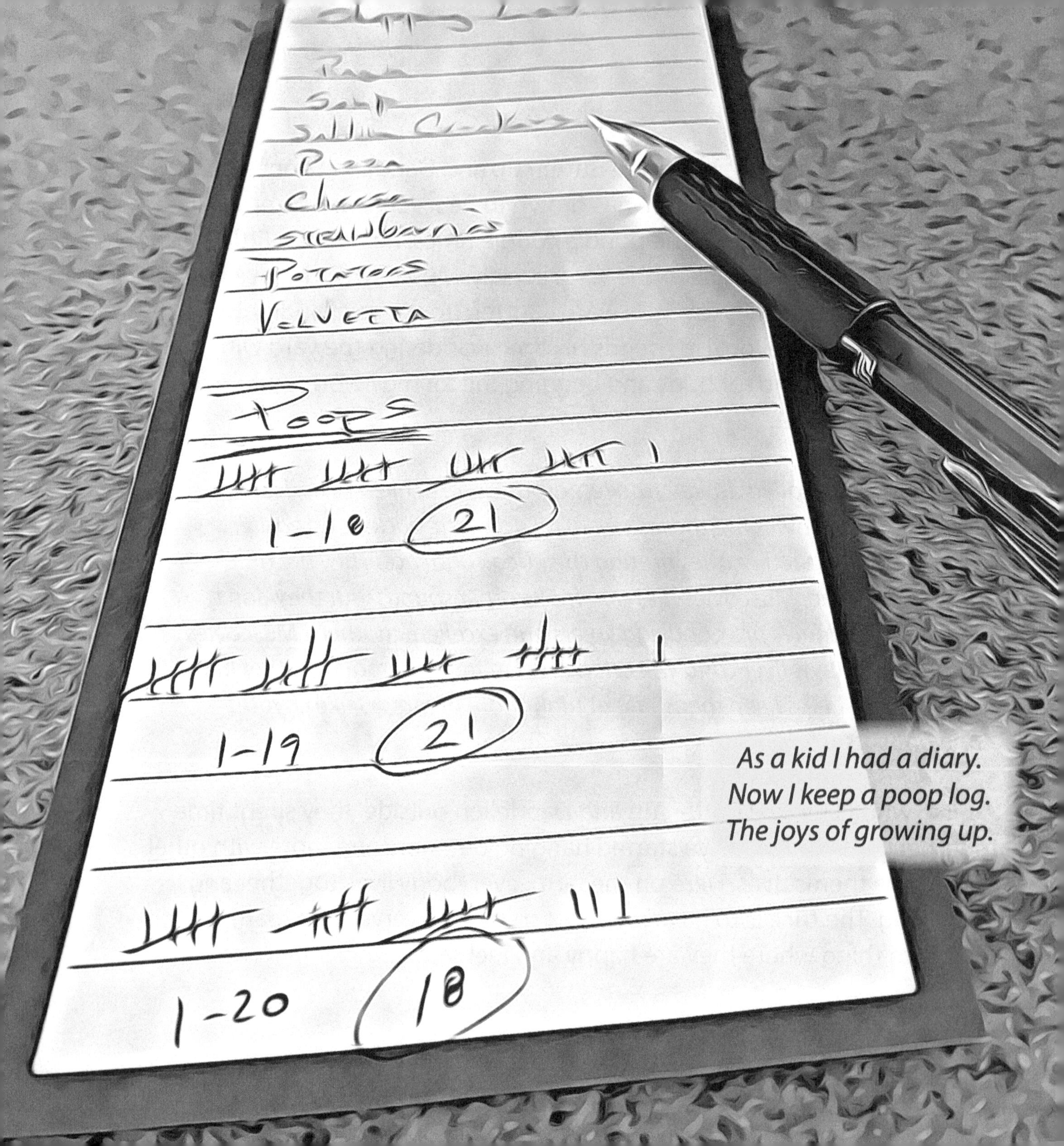

Grocery List

Bread
Salt
Saltine Crackers
Pizza
Cheese
Strawberries
Potatoes
Velvetta

Poops

|||| |||| |||| |||| |
1-1e   (21)

|||| |||| |||| |||| |
1-19   (21)

|||| |||| |||| |||
1-20   (18)

As a kid I had a diary.
Now I keep a poop log.
The joys of growing up.

Of course, there are downfalls to having a pet chicken in the house … they poop. They poop a LOT! You really can't potty-train a chicken like you can your dog. Nor do they use a litter box like a cat.

Never thought I would be googling chicken diapers, but early on in Dandelion's stay in the house, I did just that … I googled Chicken Diapers! For me, trying to put a diaper on a chicken is a lot like trying to eat soup with a fork. If someone can explain how a chicken diaper truly attaches to said chicken and covers the bottom to catch the droppings, well, I would be interested in learning.

Maybe I got the wrong size, but I just can't make it work. Dandelion looks very fashionable wearing her chicken diaper … it stayed on about 11.3 seconds. That is our first and last experience with a chicken diaper. It's much easier just to clean up after my pet chicken as needed.

The good news about chickens: When they go to the bathroom, the urine and poop is mixed together. The have a solid dropping that is easy to clean up with a couple squares of toilet paper. Out of curiosity, I wondered just how many times a day does a chicken poop? I kept a log, tracking each time Dandelion pooped. For other curious-minded folks, they average about 20 poops a day! No carpeted floors in this house. You learn quickly to keep your eyes wide open and pay attention to where you walk when you have a house chicken. Admittedly, I have made a misstep or two! GROSS!

How do you stop a bull from charging?
Take away his credit cards.

Ever since he was little, my great nephew, Brycen, has enjoyed spending time on the farm. He is like a mini animal whisperer. The animals are drawn to him. His gentle nature even has my bull, McReid, mesmerized.

Besides helping with chores and spending time with the animals, Brycen loves to go to the creek. Here we throw rocks, climb on fallen trees and dig in the sand. Whatever we are doing, he is asking me one thousand and one questions. "Aunt Kim, how do fish know how to swim?" "Aunt Kim, why do ducks like water?" "Aunt Kim, how many stars are in the sky?" "Aunt Kim, why do the cows want like to lick my hand?" "Aunt Kim, how fast do you think I can run?" "Aunt Kim, can we go fishing?" "Aunt Kim…"

I must laugh at how many questions the kid can ask. On his first visit to the farm after Dandelion became a house chicken, Brycen helped me water the cows, feed the ducks and chickens outside, walk the dogs to the mailbox. Then we headed inside to get something to snack on. Kicking our shoes off at the door, Brycen turns around to see Dandelion standing in the hallway and he exclaims … "AUNT KIM, THERE'S A CHICKEN IN YOUR HOUSE!!" I laughed so hard it hurt. It was one thing for Brycen to see all the chickens outside; it was another to find one in the house. Around here, it's just another day on the farm. (By the way, Brycen … watch where you step.) Have you ever spent time on a farm?

Chickens love fruits, veggies,
grains, insects, and other goodies.
What do you like to eat?

December

Chickens will eat just about anything. They are not picky eaters, but there are certain foods you should avoid feeding your chickens, like garlic and other strong flavored foods. Not only are foods like this bad for your chickens, but they can also cause their eggs to have a bad flavor. I keep a scrap bucket for my chickens. Once I poured tuna juice in the scrap bucket. One of my egg customers commented that they had gotten an egg that tasted fishy. I scratched my head wondering how that could be … then I finally figured it out. Now I'm very careful as to what I put in the scrap bucket for the chickens to snack on.

You should also avoid feeding your chickens raw potato, avocado, chocolate, uncooked beans, and other items. It's always best to check what is safe or unsafe for your pets. I'm sure grilled cheese sandwiches do not fall in the good food category for chickens. Somebody needs to tell Dandelion to lay off the junk food.

Chickens are omnivores. This means they eat both plants and animal matter such as worms, insects and whatever they can catch, including mice.

What is in the salad?
How many different food items can you count?

With winter taking a good hold on Missouri once again, I'm keeping Dandelion inside most days. Green grass and bugs are non-existent right now. Time to tap into my inner chef and create some amazing salads for Dandelion to supplement her regular meals. Better step out of the way when I call Dandelion for her salad … that girl will flat out run from one end of the house to the other in 2.3 seconds to get her special salad that I have made just for her.

At the grocery store, I find myself shopping for fresh salad mix of spinach and lettuce. Then I carefully pick out the best looking carrots, blueberries, raspberries, strawberries, blackberries, corn on the cob, green beans and whatever other goodies I can find. I like to give her a variety and mix it up depending on what looks the best at the store when I'm shopping. Sometimes I add broccoli, cauliflower, fresh melons, apples, whatever fresh fruits and veggies catch my eye. I chop, slice, shred everything into bite size pieces, then as a final touch, I sprinkle a pinch of mealworms on top. I think of them as her special croutons that take her salad to a Michelin-Star level that would be the envy of chickens around the world.

I feel like a chef … a Chicken Chef. Perhaps one day they will have a "Chopped" episode on TV featuring chefs that create meals for pets. Tune in: You might see me on television sometime in the near future.

January

With the cold and snow, Dandelion has pretty much become a full-time house chicken. On nicer days, she goes out for a little, but I don't let her stay too long. The other day, it was so cold outside, Dandelion ran out the door as I opened it to let one of the dogs inside. She made it about three feet out the door and did a U-Turn. Lickity-split, Dandelion was back inside before I have a chance to close the door. She is a wise bird … maybe not as wise as an owl, but she's one smart chicken.

Seems like Dandelion has become very attached to the other animals that live in the house. She moves room-to-room as if she is keeping track of everyone. She is most settled when everybody is together in one room. The dogs, Marilyn, Lucy, and Zak don't mind sharing space with a chicken at all. You can see in this picture the wooden crate by my desk … this is where she roosts at night to sleep or when she wants to sit by me as I work at my desk. In the morning, she flies over to the purple pan which is where I keep her grain and water. She flies up here any time she's hungry or thirsty. Sometimes, Dandelion will send shavings flying all over the room as she tries to take a dust bath. Pro tip: When you have a house chicken, keep a broom and dustpan handy.

This morning while doing farm chores, I had to bust ice, haul water, and toss feed, just like any day. I was hungry and ready to get back inside to fix my breakfast. Once inside, it wasn't long before I heard Dandelion knocking at the door with her beak,. What a life for a chicken. I let her inside and went about my day. I have lots of work to do and need to get busy.

By early afternoon, I noticed things were quiet and went looking for Dandelion, who is sitting in my easy chair in the living room. I'm wondering if she will lay an egg in my chair. She hasn't laid one for several weeks now. Dandelion looked pretty comfy in my big easy chair. Next time I check on her, she is standing over a beautiful egg, freshly laid in my easy chair. Yes, this is life with a house chicken. New house motto: Watch your step, and watch where you sit. Life with a house chicken is an adventure every day. Dandelion has so much personality, she makes my heart smile.

Ours may not be your typical friendship, but it works. I cater to her every need, prepare her special treats, I even share my easy chair. Pretty good life for a chicken. At the same time, I get super fresh eggs, I'm entertained daily by her shenanigans, and I get to say that one of my best friends on earth is a chicken! I sure love that girl. Life on the farm is a dream come true. If asked who rules the roost on the farm, the answer would most definitely be DANDELION!

Adventures from Around The Farm at Hybrid Hollow: Are you wondering what happens next? Keep an eye out for more adventures to follow.

TERMS & DEFINITIONS

Chick – A baby chicken

Chore – A small or odd job; routine task.

Domestic – Animals that live alongside people. Sometimes, they are said to be tame or are considered as pets.

Down – Baby birds are covered in down feathers which are very soft and fluffy. As they grow, you will find a layer of down under their chest feathers, which helps insulate them from heat loss.

Drake – A male duck

Duckling – A baby duck

Ecosystem – an area where animals, plants, and other organisms work together with the landscape, weather, and other factors to create a bubble of life.

Flock – A group of birds that eat, rest and travel together.

Free Range – A method of farming where the animals can roam freely outdoors.

Hen – A female chicken or duck

Herd – A group of animals, such as cows, that live together.

Irish Dexter – A small, old fashioned breed of cattle from Ireland that is listed as recovering on the Livestock Conservation endangered list.

Landlubber – Nautical term for any person or animal having no experience in bodies of water, preferring to be on land.

Molting – Shedding of old feathers to make way for new growth. This happens every year in chickens. During this time, hens will stop laying eggs to build up their nutrient reserves. It can take 8-12 weeks for new feathers to grow back in.

Muscovy Duck – A large, domesticated duck with adult males weighing around 15 pounds and the females weighing around 6 pounds. They originated in Africa and South America but have become very popular in the United States, especially on small farms. Muscovies are known as the quackless duck because although they make noises, they don't quack. They are capable of flight and come in a variety of colors from white, black, chocolate and lavender. Most recognizable due to the red warts or wattles around their face, they are good egg layers and excellent mothers.

Pecking Order – A basic pattern of social organization among animals, especially chickens. The dominate animals peck other members of the flock in order to show their leadership in the group.

Rodent – Mammals that have ever-growing incisors (front teeth). This includes rats, mice, hamsters, gerbils, guinea pigs, rabbits, squirrels, and others. These animals need hard items like nuts and other materials to help keep their teeth filed down.

Roost – When a chicken goes to bed, it is called going to roost. Generally, most domestic chickens are kept in chicken houses at night to keep them safe from predators while they sleep. They seek places high off the ground to perch as they go to bed for the night or go to roost.

Rooster – A male chicken

Turken / Naked Neck Chickens – This breed of chicken lacks feathers on its neck, causing it to look like a turkey, but it is 100% pure chicken. Their unique look makes them easy to identify in a flock of chickens. They are hardy, and most hens will lay 120-150 eggs per year.

Wattle – Colored fleshy lobe(s) found on the head or neck of some domestic ducks, chickens, turkeys, and other birds.

Yolk Sac – A membrane that encloses the yolk of eggs in birds, reptiles, and marsupials. It circulates nourishment (food) from the yolk to the developing embryo and newly hatched chick or duckling. In ducks and chickens, the yolk sac provides food for the baby during the first two or three days of life.

Special thanks to my friends,

*Barb and John McCormick, for all your guidance and
hand-holding in bringing this book from a dream to reality.*

Kim grew up in the suburbs of St. Louis, Missouri. At the age of ten, she spent a summer on her grandparents' farm, which changed her life forever. From that summer on, she set her mind to having a farm of her own someday. After graduating college with a degree in Animal Science, she settled on a twenty-acre farm in mid-Missouri. She now shares her life with an assortment of critters and couldn't be happier. Dreams really do come true. Learn more at www.hybridhollowproduction.com

Dandelion is a naked neck breed of chicken called a Turken. She was hatched by a duck, but chickens don't swim. Therefore, she was raised in the house by Kim and her mom, Jo. As an adult, Dandelion spends part of her day outside, weather permitting, she free ranges the farm. In the evening or in bad weather, Dandelion stays inside where she is equally at home.

Made in the USA
Monee, IL
07 March 2023

28935856R10044